THE KEY TO CHICAGO

MARTHA BENNETT KING

THE KEY TO CHICAGO

KEYS TO THE CITIES SERIES

J. B. LIPPINCOTT COMPANY

PHILADELPHIA · NEW YORK

KEYS TO THE CITIES SERIES

THE KEY TO PHILADELPHIA *by Dorothy Loder*
THE KEY TO LONDON *by Alicia Street*
THE KEY TO NEW YORK *by Alice Fleming*
THE KEY TO PARIS *by Marjory Stoneman Douglas*
THE KEY TO BOSTON *by George F. and Mildred Weston*
THE KEY TO SAN FRANCISCO *by Charlotte Jackson*
THE KEY TO ROME *by Monroe Stearns*
THE KEY TO VIENNA *by Raymond A. Wohlrabe and Werner E.*
Krusch
THE KEY TO CHICAGO *by Martha Bennett King*

MAP BY GEORGE MCVICKER

CONTENTS

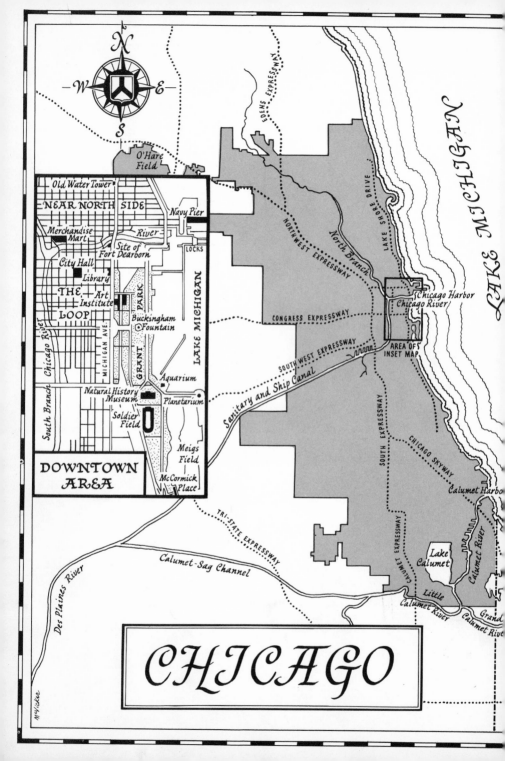

CHICAGO

1. THE WINDY CITY

CHICAGO stands tall in the heart of America with the vast blue Lake Michigan for its front yard. Flat fertile prairies fan out around it into a twelve-state Middle West. Chicago is the nation's railroad hub, its trucking center, its air crossroads. In the spring of 1959 Chicago also became a great inland seaport.

In 1959, with the opening of the Saint Lawrence Seaway, Chicago began a new chapter in its brief history. By nature it always had been a key link in the great inland waterway between the Great Lakes and the Gulf of Mexico. But with the opening of the Seaway, deep-draft ships could move directly from the Atlantic Ocean to the Port of Chicago. They could bring goods from all ports of the world and return to home ports laden with goods made in Chicago and food grown in all of the Middle Western states. The new seaport meant new wealth and new jobs for Chicago. A surge of energy seemed to sweep through the city and touch off a great celebration, "Operation Inland Sea."

On July 2, 1959, fifteen ships of the United States Navy, Task Force Forty-seven, steamed into Chicago. Thousands of sailboats darted around them like white butterflies. Pleasure cruisers, flags flying, brass gleaming, filled all city harbors. Sleek freighters and tankers moved on the horizon. On July 4, 1500 marines made a mock amphibious landing on Montrose Beach, the Navy's Blue Angels flew a daredevil circus high in the air, and 63,114 visitors swarmed through the colorful sixty-five-nation Trade Fair which covered mile-long Navy Pier.

The celebration reached a high climax on Monday, the sixth of July, when a royal yacht, the *Britannia,* sailed toward Grant Park in downtown Chicago. It carried Elizabeth II, Great Britain's young queen, and Prince Philip. They had dedicated the opening of the Saint Lawrence Seaway and were pausing to visit the new inland seaport. Chicago rolled out its red carpet. Millions of citizens lined miles of streets for the royal parade, and everyone felt a new pride in the big windy city.

Chicago had been a mere swamp-cradled baby on the shores of the lake in 1833. One hundred and twenty-six years later it had become a handsome young giant, second largest city in the United States, third largest in the western world. It had grown up to be a big-business big-industry city; a world-fair-convention city; a city with famous museums, libraries, and universities; a city

BUCKINGHAM FOUNTAIN IN GRANT PARK

whose calendar was crowded with colorful events.

Summer sight-seeing boats still take visitors into the lake to see "the Queen's view of Chicago." The skyscraper skyline behind banks of trees in Grant Park looks like a great painted stage set. Geyserlike cascades of spray rise from Buckingham Fountain. Four pairs of gigantic bronze sea horses, honoring four states that border Lake Michigan, stand in the fountain, spouting 15,700 gallons of water each minute during major displays.

To the south, the Chicago Natural History Museum, inspired by a temple in Greece, heads the broad drive which sweeps past the fountain. Shedd Aquarium flashes white in the sun. The pillars of Soldier Field, an open stadium for festivals and sports events, shine through the trees.

A tree-lined drive connects Grant Park with Northerly Island. Adler Planetarium and Astronomical Museum shares the Island with Meigs Field, the world's largest single-run airport. Hundreds of small planes land and take off every day from this field by the lake.

By day, Chicago lives up to her title, *Urbs in Horto,* "City in a Garden." The Latin words appear on the great seal that stamps all city documents. By night, Chicago is "Queen of the

Lakes," so sparkling with lights that she seems to be wearing a treasure in rubies and emeralds and diamonds. To the south, flames from the steel mills, Chicago's own fireworks, light up the sky.

More than eighteen million visitors arrive in Chicago each year from all parts of the world. Many study in universities and special schools. Others take part in big fairs or consult doctors in the city's great medical centers.

Twelve hundred or more conventions are held in Chicago each year. Bankers, bakers, doctors, toolmakers, nuclear scientists, housewives, 4-H Clubs, and countless organizations meet in the city. Ten Democratic and thirteen Republican national conventions have been held in Chicago.

Boat shows, auto shows, antique and hobby shows, sportsmen's shows, Junior Achievement fairs, International Livestock and horse shows, American Indian shows, and Ice Capades are held in the city's hotels, stadiums, and marts. Chicago's newest convention hall, McCormick Palace, at Twenty-third Street on the lake, opened in December 1960. Named for the late Colonel Robert R. McCormick, publisher of the Chicago *Tribune,* its ten-acre roof covers restaurants, theaters, display rooms, huge galleries and halls.

Many visitors ride to the "Top of the Rock,"

BEACHES MARK CHICAGO'S TWENTY-SIX MILES OF SHORELINE. THE OAK STREET BEACH ON THE NEAR NORTH SIDE

the glass-enclosed top of the forty-one-story Prudential Building for a four-sided view of the city. There they see a forest of glass, steel, and stone buildings rising beside the great sheet of Lake Michigan's sparkling blue water that spreads to the north and the east.

A wide Outer Drive, flanked by beaches and walls of stone block, curves with the lake's shore. More than 200 parks make islands of green throughout the city.

To the west, a golden smoke haze from millions of chimneys hovers above miles of factories and houses. Chicago's own city limits stretch twenty-

six miles on the lake front and fan ten miles inland to north, west, and south, where it forms
miles of suburbs and villages.

Planes soar overhead for a landing at Midway
Airport, southwest of the city, or at O'Hare International Airport, northwest of the city. Midway is
known as the busiest airport in the world. A plane
lands or departs every minute of the day and night,
and 10,000,000 passengers go through the port
every year. O'Hare is the largest airport in the
world and may soon steal the title of "busiest"
from Midway. It is making plans to handle
30,000,000 passengers a year by 1970.

A network of highways, expressways, canals, and

THE FLOOD-LIGHTED WRIGLEY, FAR RIGHT, THE BEACON ON THE PALM-
OLIVE BUILDING, AND THE OUTER DRIVE

Hedrich-Blessing

steel rails leads into the heart of Chicago. Every second of the day and night a dozen or more trucks, planes, and boats enter or leave Chicago. They carry wheat, corn, and livestock; oil, iron, steel, coal, and gas; spruce and pine from northern forests; newsprint from Canada; packaged foods, clothing, machinery, and all kinds of luxuries.

Freighters and tankers move through the lake to dock beside Navy Pier or to enter the Chicago River, lined with newspaper plants, warehouses, modern office buildings, the Merchandise Mart, the forty-two-story Civic Opera Building, railroad stations, and a big United States Post Office.

The Chicago River, shaped like a "Y," flows away from the lake and divides the city into north, west, and south sections. Dozens of bridges part in the middle and rise to let even a tall-masted sailboat pass. Motorboats, sailboats, sight-seeing boats, fire and police boats wait with barges, freighters, and tugs to pass through a single lock, 600 feet long by 80 feet wide, that separates lake and river. Watching boats come and go, even Chicagoans say, "Where is the Port of Chicago?" One part of the port lies south of the city in Calumet Harbor, where tugs guide big ships through the Calumet River, which twists among steel mills and refineries. The downtown part of the port includes Navy Pier and docks along the Chicago River.

Loaded barges move along the south branch of the river into the Sanitary and Ship Canal, and into the Des Plaines and Illinois rivers. These rivers flow into the Mississippi River, which flows to the Gulf of Mexico. By inland waterway alone, Chicago is in touch with cities as far apart as New Orleans and Minneapolis; Brownsville, Texas, and Sioux City, Iowa.

Many visitors who see Chicago from the "Rock" or a ship or the Outer Drive say that the city has one of the most beautiful faces on earth. But those who enter Chicago by train say that Chicago has the smoke-stained face of an industrial giant.

Colorful contrasts are a mark of Chicago. The lake front, the tall buildings of the Loop, and the elegant apartment buildings on the Gold Coast make one part of the city. Factories, miles of comfortable family homes, even slums make up other parts of Chicago. Sight-seeing buses that start from the Loop offer visitors many different views of the sprawling city.

The Loop, in downtown Chicago, takes its name from the loop made by elevated-train tracks that enclose an area five blocks wide by seven blocks long. The tracks follow Wabash, Lake,

Wells, and Van Buren streets, and Chicagoans
who come from the north, west, and south sides of
the city talk about "riding around the Loop" or
"shopping in the Loop."

Chicago's biggest department stores are in the
Loop. Marshall Field and Company's big store
faces State Street, as do Carson Pirie Scott & Co.,
Chas. A. Stevens, Wieboldt's, Goldblatt's, the Fair,
and Sears Roebuck. Smaller retail stores, selling
everything from books and candy to refrigerators
and fur coats, share the Loop with banks, theaters,
restaurants, and tall office buildings. Beautiful
displays in store windows draw thousands of sight-
seers, as well as shoppers who may spend over two
million dollars a day in State Street stores alone.
The corner of State and Madison streets is said to
be the busiest in the world.

The size of everything in Chicago surprises
many sight-seers. The three thousand-room Hil-
ton Hotel is the biggest in the world. The Merchandise Mart is the world's biggest commercial
building, Grant Park's underground garage is the
largest in the world, with space for 2400 cars. Chicago has the biggest printing plant in the world,
the biggest cheese factory, the biggest aquarium,
the biggest conservatory for flowers. It even has
one of the biggest American flags in the world.

STATE STREET IN THE 1960S

The flag, cut from four thousand square yards of cloth, hangs from ceiling to ground floor in Marshall Field's store on patriotic holidays.

Sight-seeing buses move across the river to the Near North Side, an area extending from the river to North Avenue and from the lake to the north branch of the river. Millionaires' castles once lined the Gold Coast, the drive along the lake, but today tall apartment buildings have taken their place.

Many beautiful old homes still stand on streets just west of the Drive, but farther west many blocks of old houses which have become "expen-

sive slums" are being torn down to make way for modern buildings.

The Near North Side claims Rush Street, with its many night clubs, as well as fashionable stores and big churches. Moody Bible Institute and Newberry Library, one of the great libraries of the world, stand on the Near North Side.

The tree-lined "Magnificent Mile" stretches from the old Water Tower at Chicago Avenue to the river. The old-fashioned, castellated Water Tower marked Chicago's limits in 1871 and was one of the few buildings to defy the great fire. The water pumps in the station across from the Tower were put out of commission early in the fire, but its smoke-stained stone walls still stand and the whir of new machinery is heard by passers-by. Both buildings are cherished as landmarks.

The lake once washed onto beaches near the Water Tower, but today buses must drive east to the lake on "made land." Three big hospitals, Northwestern University's downtown school, the "glass houses" designed by Mies van der Rohe, the Furniture Mart, and the many buildings from Oak Street to Navy Pier all stand on "made land."

"Made land" also gave Chicago its downtown show place, Grant Park. Through the years Chicago has made over 1600 acres of land for itself by

THE OLD CHICAGO WATER TOWER

North Michigan Avenue Association

pushing back the waters of the lake.

As sight-seeing buses head for the "Near South Side," they pass the big housing developments, known as Lake Meadows and Prairie Shores, that have taken the place of acres of slums between Twenty-third, and Thirty-fifth streets.

In Chinatown bus drivers point out the Ling Long Museum, which tells of five thousand years of Chinese history, the only museum of its kind in the United States. Near Thirty-fifth Street, buses pause at the great stone gates of Union Stock Yard, symbol of the slaughter and meat-packing industry that brought early wealth to Chicago and gave it the name of "hog butcher." The Amphitheater in the Stockyards is the scene of annual horse shows and 4-H Club expositions. The Sirloin Room in the old Stock Yard Inn is famed for its steaks.

Today slaughterhouses have moved farther west, and Packingtown is falling down. The slums, "Back of the Yards," also have gone. Crime once was so fierce there that businessmen were afraid to hire a man or boy whose address was in that area. But in 1939 the people formed themselves into a council to get rid of rats, garbage, rotting houses, gangsters, and crooked politicians. Today they have a neat and trim workingmen's town with good schools and playgrounds for all.

West of the Loop buses go slowly along Maxwell Street, where dozens of languages can be heard and where everything from cookies to coats is sold from pushcarts and stands on the street.

Chicago has its Italian, Polish, Russian, Hungarian, Irish, and German communities. It has its Swedish, Chinese, Japanese, and Negro commmunities. Puerto Ricans, Mexicans, and whites from the southern mountains are the most recent new-

LAKE MEADOWS AND PRAIRIE SHORES APARTMENTS
Photo by Godfrey Lundberg, Chicago Historical Society

comers to the city. These people think of themselves as Chicagoans, but they also treasure their
ancient songs, dances, stories, festivals, foods, and
customs.

Many communities hold colorful festivals, dra-
gon parades, and street fairs each year. Christmas
trees, decorated in traditional ways by thirty or
more national groups, are on display at the Museum of Science and Industry each holiday season.

On the Far South Side buses pass the Museum
of Science and Industry in Jackson Park, where
the World's Columbian Exposition was held in
1893. They move on along the "Midway," which
connects Jackson and Washington parks, past International House and the Gothic towers of the
University of Chicago.

The Midway is now two boulevards separated
by deep, grassy hollows. During the Columbian
Exposition it was one long lagoon, and Venetian
gondolas floated past restaurants and exhibition
buildings.

The Columbian Exposition was one of the most
spectacular fairs in history. Millions of visitors
from all parts of the world walked through its
buildings, stared at the displays of newfangled
electric lights, marveled at scientific inventions,
and rode on the huge Ferris wheel, whose thirty-

six cars circled 265 feet into the air. Such a wheel had never before been seen in America. No visitor ever forgot it.

It was the Columbian Exposition which gave Chicago its nickname of "Windy City." The name did not come from the wind but from the boasting and outspoken pride of its citizens.

The United States Congress had voted to hold a multi-million-dollar world's fair in honor of the four hundredth anniversary of Columbus's discov-

MCCORMICK PLACE, THE EXPOSITION CENTER OVERLOOKS BURNHAM HARBOR AND MEIGS FIELD

Chicago Tribune

ery of America. New York, St. Louis, and Washington all wanted the fair. Chicago, the youngest
and boldest of cities, also put in a bid. It claimed
it could build a magnificent fair on deserted sand
dunes eight miles south of the river. Architects
from eastern cities said it could not be done.

"Don't pay any attention to the nonsensical
claims of that windy city," Charles Dana wrote in
the New York *Sun*. "Its people couldn't build a
World's Fair if they won it."

Chicago won the big fair and made good its
boast, but Chicago's breezes still remind visitors
that Chicago might very well have earned its nickname from the wind itself. "Hold your hat when
you go to Chicago," folks say. "The wind is a
trickster." In summer, gentle breezes suddenly
shift and flip boats upside down. In winter, wind
sweeps even men off their feet. Ropes have to be
strung around buildings to help pedestrians get
around corners. On a rampage, the wind whips
flags from their poles, tears awnings, and smashes
huge plate-glass windows. It crashes the lake's
waves onto beaches, sending spray flying over long
lines of cars which creep bumper to bumper along
the Outer Drive.

Chicago's tall buildings are built to sway like
great trees in the wind. New buildings sway six

to seven inches, but older ones sway as much as twelve inches.

The weather is aso a trickster in Chicago. On a breathless, hot summer day, the temperature can suddenly drop thirty degrees. On a dry-as-a-bone day in winter, a handful of snowflakes can turn into a car-stalling blizzard within thirty minutes.

The lake keeps Chicago's temperatures moderate most of the year, but the thermometer can stand close to one hundred degrees five or more days at a time in midsummer, and drop below zero in winter. "Chicago has no spring," many say. "You jump out of the refrigerator into the fire."

As sight-seeing buses return to the Loop, many visitors laughingly admit that they half expected to see gangsters with sawed-off shotguns all over Chicago. Stories of Scarface Al Capone, Dillinger, and the liquor-running hoodlums of the 1920s have spread over the world and given the city a tough, lawless reputation. And it will be many years before the gangster legends fade.

There is still crime in Chicago, but Chicagoans constantly search for ways to control it. They tackle the job with the same restless energy that marked the city when it earned the name "Windy City."

Chicagoans are accused of boasting about their

city at the drop of a hat, but they also never stop criticizing. No visitor can make as many remarks about the things that are wrong with Chicago as Chicagoans themselves can make.

2. JOBS AND MORE JOBS

It is easy to discover how Chicagoans earn a living today. The sights and sounds of big business and industry fill the air. Short blasts of boat whistles say that ships passing through Chicago's harbors carry more tonnage than ships going through the Suez and Panama canals combined. A flash of fire from the steel mills says, "Chicago is top maker of steel, top U.S. maker of diesel engines and railroad equipment."

Smoke rising from 15,000 factories says, "Chicago is number one U.S. maker of candy, of paint, of circus-tent tops, of athletic and sports goods, of ball and roller bearings. It is the number one maker of telephone equipment, food machinery, metal parts, tools, and dies."

It is hard to name a machine that Chicago doesn't make. It boasts of making the first Pull-

man car, the first refrigerator, the first washing machine.

Variety of business and industry has helped Chicago to grow big and prosperous. Chicago's classified telephone directory lists more than three thousand types of business and 200,000 places of business. Nineteen hundred trade, labor, and business associations have headquarters in Chicago. The American Medical Association, the National Congress of Parents and Teachers, and the American Library Association also have their headquarters in Chicago.

Chicago is the capital of the electronics industry, making parts for radio and TV sets, for radar and broadcasting equipment. Chicago is the packaging center of the world, the number one maker of tin cans, of paper, fiber, and plastic containers. It is the second-largest manufacturing and processing center for plastics. It makes everything from football helmets to cases for jet interceptor planes.

The gilded statue of Ceres, goddess of grain, is a symbol of Chicago's role as the world's largest grain-trading center. Ceres stands 31 feet 6 inches high on top of the Board of Trade Building, looking off to the farmlands, and down into La Salle Street, Chicago's banking and financial center.

THE BOARD OF TRADE

Photo by Americo Grasso, Chicago Historical Society

Each year many thousands of visitors go to the Board of Trade to watch trading in the "pits." There men buy and sell without words. They use a sign language of fingers and clenched fists to confirm sales worth hundreds of thousands of dollars. They sell millions of bushels of grain that is not even cut from the fields. Such sales are called "futures." Restaurants, bakeries, hotels, and wholesale food firms send men to buy "future" carloads of wheat, corn, soybeans, eggs, butter, poultry, onions, potatoes, and fruit.

THE MERCHANDISE MART

Along the north branch of the Chicago River, Montgomery Ward's store is marked by a statue of a winged messenger. Sears Roebuck, Butler Brothers, Alden, and many smaller firms make Chicago the mail-order capital of the world. Forty million catalogs are sent out of Chicago each year to homes all over the world.

Chicago is a world wholesale-marketing center. Eleven thousand two hundred and fifty wholesale dealers carry some 30,000 different items, from electrical goods, drugs, lumber, and hardware to paper, foods, and machinery of all kinds.

One of the striking symbols of Chicago's wholesale power is the Merchandise Mart, which commands a superb view of the city from the fork of the river. Opened in 1930, the Mart is known as the greatest wholesale buying center in the world, as well as the largest commercial building. It is a true giant's showroom, covering two city blocks, rising twenty-five stories in the air at the tower. It has ninety-five acres of floor space, seven and one-half miles of corridors. Eleven hundred and ten firms rent space in the Mart, displaying some 1,209,000 separate items made by 3900 manufacturers. A 700-page guide is issued twice a year to help buyers find everything from bicycles and carpets to furniture and lamp shades. The Mart is a small city in itself. Over thirty thousand people work there each day. Each year some five hundred thousand store owners and buyers visit trade shows and purchase goods there. For a small fee, trained guides take visitors through the most beautiful exhibits, but no one can buy in the Mart without a card that entitles him to buy at wholesale prices.

Acres of storage space are needed for all the goods that are manufactured in Chicago, and for all the farm produce that is moved in and out of the city. Chicago has great refrigerated storage space and a large amount of general-merchandise storage space. Thousands of brightly painted trucks wait by warehouses to move all the goods that are bought and sold in Chicago. Refrigerated trucks carry fresh and frozen foods. Vans roll with dry freight. Tank trucks carry chemicals, milk, and petroleum. Diesel tractors haul long flat-bed trailers loaded with steel. Open-topped trailers carry cattle and grain.

Ten thousand motor-freight trucks move through Chicago's big terminals each day. They carry goods to more than thirty-five thousand communities. Trucks form a partnership with railroads and ships. A loaded trailer left on the dock in Calumet Harbor is lifted onto the deck of a freighter. When it reaches its destination, it is lifted ashore and towed away. Railroads take loaded trucks "piggy-back."

Chicago has eight thousand miles of track that forms an inner and outer belt for the city. Two hundred seven thousand cars can be parked at one time. Thirty-five thousand boxcars, flatcars, oil and refrigerator cars move in and out of Chicago each day. They load and unload at two hundred and twenty-five freight houses. Cars are shunted by gravity, controlled by automatic retarders, coupled into long trains, and sent off through the country.

"It all means jobs," Chicago says proudly. Dredging, tunneling, shoveling jobs; lifting, heaving, and building jobs; buying, selling, wrapping, and carting jobs; bookkeeping and banking jobs; advertising, designing, and printing jobs; jobs for artists, musicians, and entertainers; for pilots, drivers, engineers, scientists, and teachers; for policemen, firemen, repairmen, nurses, and politicians; for cooks, waiters, and hotelkeepers.

A marketing-shipping center attracts more and more industry. Industry attracts workers. Workers bring families. More industries spring up to serve more and more families.

3. HOME-TOWN CHICAGO

NEARLY four million persons live in Chicago's city limits. Two million more live in six counties that form the great Chicago metropolitan area. Two hundred and seventy-five villages and towns join Chicago so closely that often only policemen and mayors know which line is which. Over three fourths of a million people who live outside city limits commute to Chicago each working day by car, train, subway, or bus.

Chicago's downtown area, in and near the Loop, is the show place and big-business heart of the city. The rest of Chicago is a collection of communities that join one another so closely that they seem like one endless city.

People often say, "I live in Hyde Park, or Rogers Park, or Bridgeport, or Austin." As Chicago grew bigger, spreading away from the mouth of the river, it swallowed up other small prairie villages. Those villages still keep their old names and the names even appear on city tax bills. Families are proud that their parents and grandparents lived in small Illinois villages that became part of Chicago.

Chicago is a family town. Millions of Chicagoans live in one- or two-story brick or frame houses on long tree-lined streets that seem like those of small towns anywhere. Children play up and down the street. Grownups sit on the porch, lean on the fences to talk to their neighbors, work in their gardens, wash their own cars, hang out the washing, and paint their own houses.

Many communities have their own shops, schools, churches, branch libraries, and community centers. Some people spend all their lives within a few blocks of their homes. They will say, "I haven't set foot in the Loop for years." But most people shop in the big downtown stores, at least during holidays. They also go to the Loop for parades and big shows. They visit museums, go to a theater, and sit in Grant Park on summer nights when fine orchestras play in the Band Shell.

There are two thousand four hundred churches, synagogues, and places of worship in Chicago. One neighborhood community has seven Catholic churches, serving seven different national groups. Domes and spires of many community churches often have an old-world air in contrast to the modern architecture of Saint Peter's Church, the Methodist Temple, and the Chicago Loop Synagogue. The Synagogue's magnificent stained-glass window, 30 feet high by 40 feet long, designed by Abraham Rattner, is attracting visitors

THE SKYLINE ALONG MICHIGAN AVENUE FROM ACROSS GRANT PARK

Chicago Park District

from all parts of the world. The Rockefeller Memorial Chapel on the University of Chicago's campus, and the Bahai Temple in Wilmette also are among the architectural beauties of Chicago.

Chicagoans must like to go to school, for one out of every four persons, preschool children to grandparents, take some kind of regular school work. Counting schools and students is like taking the census.

There are eight hundred public, parochial, and Lutheran elementary schools in Chicago, one hundred and twenty-nine high schools, and hundreds of private schools. Chicago has twenty-four colleges and universities besides junior colleges, teachers' colleges, and theological schools. Young people who want to be engineers, riveters, architects, designers, bakers, barbers, watchmakers, even repairmen for television sets, go to more than two hundred technical schools. Actors, artists, and models all go to school in Chicago.

Some schools are open around the clock, so that those who work in the daytime may attend classes at night. Thousands study by television.

Chicagoans are book-minded. There are more than two hundred libraries in Chicago besides those in schools and private collections. There are special libraries for doctors, businessmen, bankers, artists, engineers, musicians, and historians.

The Chicago Public Library is a giant in itself. Its stately main building on Michigan Avenue overlooks Grant Park, but it also has fifty-five branches in various parts of the city and four mobile units (three traveling branches and a Children's Book Caravan).

Chicago has four metropolitan newspapers, Chicago's *American,* the Chicago *Daily News,* the Chicago *Sun-Times,* and the Chicago *Tribune.* Most Chicagoans read at least one of these papers, but they also read their own community's paper, or one of the many foreign-language newspapers published in the city.

Chicagoans have come from all parts of the world. Two thirds of the population belong to some thirty national groups. Earliest settlers were Yankees and Southerners who came from states on the Atlantic coast. Germans, Irish, and Swedes arrived in the 1840s and 1850s to build the canals and railroads. They did not become millionaires, but they made enough money to settle in clean and comfortable communities.

Hundreds of thousands of Czechs, Slovaks, Italians, Greeks, Russians, and Poles who reached Chicago in the 1880s and 1890s were less fortunate. They came without money. They had no special skills. They could not speak English. In Europe they had seen posters sent by land companies in Illinois. "Cheap land. Good jobs," the posters said. "Earn $1.25 a day. Buy your own farm in a very short time." But men often failed to find jobs in Chicago. They moved into decaying houses that others had deserted and never succeeded in earning enough money to find better homes. Twenty thousand people once lived in a

THE CHICAGO RIVER WITH THE CHICAGO SUN-TIMES BUILDING IN THE FOREGROUND

few blocks along Halsted Street. Their houses had no toilets and no running water. Dozens of families drew water for drinking and cooking from one well. There was no water for bathing.

When young Jane Addams saw the miserable slums along Halsted Street in 1859, she began a long fight to make life better for Chicago's helpless people. Halsted Street had once been a street of big houses with broad lawns, and Charles J. Hull's house was still standing. Jane Addams and Ellen Gates Starr moved in, and Hull House became a place where all kinds of people could find help, advice, and friends. Some of Chicago's wealthiest women joined Jane Addams. They forced city officials to collect garbage from the streets. They fought for laws which would keep women and children from working fourteen to sixteen hours a day in dark factories. They set up playgrounds and a nursery school where working mothers could leave their youngest children. They opened classes in Hull House where men and women could learn to speak English and where boys could learn trades which would help them find jobs. They helped establish Chicago's first juvenile court, so that boys who had committed minor crimes would not be judged with old and hard criminals.

Jane Addams died in May 1935, but Hull House still stands, one of thirty-three members of the Chicago Federation of Settlements and Neighborhood Centers.

4. FUN IN CHICAGO

"YOU DON'T have to be rich to have fun in Chicago," families say. Anyone can swim in the lake or play on the beaches or fish from stone walls. The Chicago Park District has seven harbors with hundreds of moorings and stalls for motor and sailboats. There is such a long waiting list for regular moorings that many keep a boat in the garage and take it to water on a trailer.

Ten to twenty miles from the heart of the city there is a ring of forest preserves with 46,000 acres of forest, meadows, and lakes. One map lists ninety-six different wooded areas for picnics, camping, and fishing. It shows one hundred and seventy-five miles of hiking and bicycling trails, with open grasslands for sports and special centers for nature study. Rolling sand dunes along the lake north of the city have been turned into a

1600-acre state park, a botanical wonderland. Fox, deer, coyote, muskrat, weasel, beaver, and badger still roam the preserves. Horned owls, blue herons, and egrets still live undisturbed.

Chicago has two hundred and seventeen parks and play yards with programs that list hundreds of activities from ballet and square dancing to bird watching and cattle raising. Three million boys and girls go to the Park District's seventy-three day camps. Twelve thousand baseball teams and six thousand softball teams meet regularly in the parks.

Chicagoans not only like to take part in sports, they're noisy fans of professional sports. Chicago has two major-league baseball teams, the White Sox and the Chicago Cubs, and one professional football team, the Chicago Bears. Fans pack Comisky Park to watch the White Sox play, and move into Wrigley Field to watch the Cubs play home games.

Chicago's ice-hockey team, the Black Hawks, were contenders for the 1959 Stanley Cup. The Mackinac sailboat race, which starts from Chicago, is the longest fresh-water race in the world. There is an annual Golden Gloves boxing tournament in Chicago, as well as horse races and six-day bicycle races.

Chicago Tribune

THE MATCH LIGHTING CEREMONY

Men in Chicago have long memories for sports. A boy going to a football game with his grandfather is likely to be reminded that "the only time the Army-Navy game was ever played west of the Appalachian mountains was in Chicago's Soldier Field. One hundred and eleven thousand persons saw that game. The score was 21-21."

No sports fan will ever forget the Pan-American games held in Chicago in August 1959. Twenty-four hundred competitors from twenty-seven nations took part in some three hundred different sports events from basketball and track to horse jumping and the marathon.

Boy Scouts relayed the flaming torch, symbol of good will among the participating nations, from Mexico City, site of the last games, to Soldier Field in Chicago. Ronald Rodriguez, age fifteen, whose

mother and father had moved to Chicago from
Mexico, carried the torch on its last lap.

Religious festivals and dramatic military displays also are held in Soldier Field. The Chicago-
land Music Festival is held in August each year.
Bands and choruses from schools far and wide com-
pete for a chance to appear in the festival. Nearly
one hundred thousand visitors pack the stands on
the gala night. A sight that everyone waits for is

THE MUSEUM OF SCIENCE AND INDUSTRY

Museum of Science and Industry

the match-lighting ceremony. At a signal everyone in the stands lights a match. For one moment
the darkness seems enchanted.

The Museum of Science and Industry claims
more visitors each year than any museum in the
world. Boys and girls can go down into a real,
working coal mine, watch baby chicks hatch out of
their shells, visit a captured German submarine,
look at themselves on color television, and walk
through a magnified, pulsating human heart, all
in one afternoon. This is a "do-it-yourself"
museum, where one push of a button sets exhibits
in motion to explain scientific marvels. Scientists
are as interested as ordinary visitors in the chemi-
cal, electronic, and mechanical exhibitions.

The George F. Harding Museum has a special
lure for boys. It houses a famous collection of
armor and weapons inside a stone castle. Life-
sized figures of men in armor sit astride great
horses wearing bright trappings and armor. Boys
also like to visit the Viking ship in Lincoln Park.
It is the actual ship that carried Captain Magnus
Andersen and fourteen sailors across the ocean
from Norway to the Columbian Exposition in
Chicago in 1893.

Brookfield Zoo claims that it is "just a kangaroo
jump away" from Chicago's Loop. It has more

than two thousand three hundred rare mammals, birds, reptiles, and amphibians, living in natural surroundings. The one hundred and seventy-six-acre zoo has no bars to separate animals and visitors, only wide moats or canals. In the Children's Zoo anyone can pet the baby elephant, hold a live turtle or a baby lamb.

There is also a children's zoo in the twenty-five-acre Lincoln Park Zoo near the heart of the city. There a small capuchin monkey steals caps, purses, balloons, even wrist watches, if owners aren't careful. Lincoln Park claims the first "zoo-rookery" for flightless birds. The great ape, Bushman, made his home in the zoo before he died. Now he lives, stuffed, in the Chicago Natural History Museum, while four young gorillas, Sinbad, Rajah, Lotus, and Irwin Young, draw visitors to Lincoln Park.

There are so many places to go and so many things to see in Chicago that it's hard to know where to go first. The John G. Shedd Aquarium, largest in the world, has one hundred and thirty-eight lighted tanks with ten thousand reptiles and fish from over the world. A specially built railroad car, the Nautilus, brings everything from angel-fish to sharks into the aquarium.

Visitors to Adler Planetarium watch planets

and stars move in a man-made sky. A machine projects the world of outer space onto a specially constructed ceiling. The positions of sun, moon, and stars at any past or future date in history can be shown. A collection of ancient sundials and precision instruments shows how men navigated in early times.

Young Chicagoans like to pat the tails of the two huge bronze lions that guard the Art Institute of Chicago. But the lions gaze far down Michigan Avenue, ignoring the 1,300,000 visitors who walk into the museum each year. The paintings, sculpture, drawings, and treasures in the Art Institute, valued at more than $150,000,000, actually are guarded by an electronic brain that detects both thieves and fires.

In spring Chicagoans turn out to see the flowering bushes and shrubs that turn Grant Park into one huge bouquet. Sight-seers drive west of the city to visit the eight hundred-acre Morton Arboretum. The park holds species of trees and plants from all over the world. Lombard, Illinois, near Chicago, boasts that three hundred varieties of lilacs and 75,000 tulips bloom in Lilacia Park each spring. Year round, crowds visit seasonal flower shows of chrysanthemums, lilies, poinsettias, and tulips in Garfield Park's conservatory, the

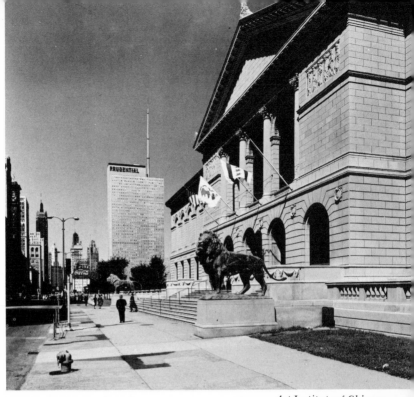

Art Institute of Chicago

THE ART INSTITUTE OF CHICAGO

largest in the world. Economic House in the conservatory shows all kinds of food-bearing bushes
and trees, from coffee and cocoa to banana and
lemon.

Outdoor art fairs are popular in Chicago. The
Fifty-seventh Street Fair, near the University of
Chicago, draws huge crowds every year. The
North Side's Old Town Art Fair draws 50,000 or
more people, who pay fifty cents admission. Local

artists and craftsmen sell paintings, sculpture, ceramics, and hand-crafted articles of all kinds. Thousands of dollars raised at an auction are used by Old Town to help support a year-round art school and gallery, a boy's club, an old people's center, and Chicago's educational television station, WTTW.

Sooner or later most visitors pause beside the river at the Michigan Avenue Bridge. It is the place where Chicago was born. A bas-relief on the bridge portrays Louis Joliet, Father Marquette, La Salle, and Tonti, the first white men to see Chicago. Another portrays a massacre. At the south end of the bridge, bronze plaques in the sidewalks mark the outlines of early Fort Dearborn.

Looking east toward the lake, it is easy to dream of the short time ago when there was no big city by the twisting green river; when there was no hum of car tires, no blasts of boat whistles; when there was only the rushing of wind and the crashing of waves on the dunes.

5. A CROSSING

Long before white men discovered Lake Michigan, Indians followed the Great Sauk Trail from Canada to Rock Island in Illinois. The trail crossed the Sauganash portage between the sluggish Chicago River and the faster-moving Des Plaines River.

The last glacier that scooped out the Great Lakes left a low continental divide eight miles south of Chicago. From there the Des Plaines River flowed toward the Gulf of Mexico, while the Chicago River flowed north and east toward Lake Michigan. In flood times the two rivers joined. In dry seasons canoes had to be carried four to nine miles through marshes and mud.

Some say that the river Chicago was named for the stinking wild onions that grew on its banks, but Indian tribes used the name of Chicago for anything powerful. Thunder, the Mississippi River, famous Indian chiefs, and the strong-smelling skunk all bore the title.

Early maps spell Chicago in many ways: Chekakou, Chigakou, and Checagou. Each tried to spell out the word as the Indians spoke it.

It was 1673 before white men left records of finding the river Chicago. That year Louis Joliet, a French-Canadian explorer, and Father Jacques Marquette, a Jesuit priest, left Green Bay in present Wisconsin to seek for a great inland river which might lead to China.

They reached the Mississippi and moved down its waters to the mouth of the Arkansas River. There they learned that the river as well as lands south to the Gulf of Mexico were claimed by the Spaniards. Turning back, the two men were guided into the Illinois River. From there, Indians eagerly showed them the well-worn Sauk Trail, the Des Plaines River, the Sauganash portage, and the river Chicago, which flowed to Lake Michigan. Indians called the big lake "The Lake of the Illinois."

Joliet and Marquette were not only excited about the beautiful country they passed through, they knew that they had discovered an important trade route for New France.

"It needs only one short canal to be cut through the portage so that boats may easily pass from river to river," Joliet said as he drew careful maps.

He set off for Quebec to give the good news to Count Frontenac, but near Montreal his canoe overturned and all maps were lost. Joliet redrew them from memory, but enemies at the French court refused to believe them. Joliet found himself caught in a war between the rulers of New France and Jesuit priests. The priests, who wished to save Indian souls, opposed the French rulers, who wished only to grow rich, and who willingly set Indians to fighting one another.

Joliet's pleas to head a new expedition and to build a canal were ignored. But three years later a nobleman, Robert René Cavelier, Sieur de La Salle, who came to be known as La Salle, was sent to explore the wilderness rivers.

Meanwhile Father Marquette, who had preached to the Illinois Indians till December 1674, became seriously ill. He started back north but could travel no farther than the Chicago portage. Indians built him a shelter of bark, gave him buffalo robes, and searched for "the Mole," a trader who knew of herb medicines. He visited the camp, but his herbs did not cure the good Father Marquette.

A PLACQUE ON THE MICHIGAN AVENUE BRIDGE COMMEMORATES MARQUETTE'S EXPLORATION OF THE CHICAGO RIVER

Winter hunger lay on the land. Deep snows made hunting impossible. Even animals starved. One day a group of strange Indians visited the camp, offering to trade much-needed corn for gunpowder. Father Marquette refused, saying that he had come only to preach, not to give powder for wars.

In the spring Indians lifted Father Marquette into a canoe and set out for the north. Near Ludington, Michigan, the gentle priest died, but the legend of his brotherliness lingered long at the portage.

La Salle moved into the wilderness wearing a long velvet coat with lace cuffs, a plumed hat, and shoes with big silver buckles. Unlike Marquette, he willingly gave gunpowder to all who would fight British traders and their Indian allies.

A PLACQUE ON THE MICHIGAN AVENUE BRIDGE COMMEMORATES LA SALLE'S EXPLORATION OF THE CHICAGO RIVER

Ignoring routes named by Joliet, La Salle left Green Bay and crossed the big lake to what is now Saint Joseph, Michigan. From there he explored to the south. It was not long until he found that the Sauganash portage and the river Chicago were, indeed, the best route, but he still tried to prove that Joliet's dream of a link between Lake Michigan and the rivers that flowed south was a foolish one.

"Even if a channel were dug at great expense," he wrote in a letter, "a sand bar would form at the mouth of the river." He added that the river itself was only serviceable fifteen to twenty days of each year; that storms on the lake were too treacherous for fur-traders' boats; that travelers often lost all of their goods as they leaped from canoes to keep them from smashing to bits on the shore; that a pack-horse route to the south would be much better than one that required boats. But in spite of efforts to discredit Joliet's plans, La Salle could not resist saying, "One day a great city will rise at the portage."

Nine years after La Salle was murdered by his own men in 1687, Jesuit priests returned to the Chicago River to build the mission of the Guardian Angel. Two villages of Miami stood near the portage, each with one hundred and fifty wigwams and huts.

It was a desolate spot. Wind swept the dunes. Black-headed gulls and kittiwakes screamed and dived into the waves that pounded the shore. On the prairies wild rice and grass grew above a man's head. A fourteen-year-old boy traveling with a party of explorers was lost as canoes were pushed through Mud Lake. When he found his way back to the mission, thirteen days later, he was ill from exposure.

The mission was closed in 1701 and Fox warriors drove the Miami away. For sixty years or more British and French traders, in fierce competition for the fur trade, kept their Indian allies fighting for control of the river and crossing.

France lost her long war with England and gave up all lands east of the Mississippi River in the

1763 Treaty of Paris. Redcoats moved into the wilderness forts and ruled even the desolate Sauganash portage.

During the Revolutionary War England lost control of the Ohio and Mississippi valley forts to the colonials, and the lonely Chicago crossing was once again left to the Indians. However, in spite of treaties, the British held onto their Great Lakes forts from Mackinac to Detroit, and continued to urge their Indian friends to make war on both American settlers and fur traders.

The day General Anthony Wayne defeated the Indians at the Battle of Fallen Timbers was an important one for Chicago. In the 1795 treaty that followed, the Indians gave to the United States many pieces of land, including "one piece six miles square at the mouth of the Chicago River where a fort formerly stood."

No white man had ever seen such a fort, but the United States government was urged to erect one to protect settlers who would move into the new Northwest Territory.

Only one man lived at the portage, a French-speaking Negro, Jean Baptiste Point du Sable. His Indian wife helped him trade pork, flour, tobacco, red and blue cloth, ostrich feathers, axes, and hoes for Indian furs. Du Sable has been called Chicago's first resident merchant.

Legends says that Du Sable's big house of logs on the north bank of the river was filled with fine paintings and beautiful furniture. He had two barns, a bakehouse, a smokehouse, a horse mill, and a workshop with many tools. He had mules, thirty head of cattle, hogs, and chickens.

In 1803 Du Sable sold his house to a trader, Le Mai, and disappeared with his family as mysteriously as he had come to the portage.

Many pleasant-sounding street names in Chicago are reminders of Indian days. Black Hawk, Caldwell, Sauganash, Wabansia, and Winnemac are named for Indian chiefs.

Hiawatha, Minnehaha, and Nokomis, Indians named in Longfellow's poem, have streets named for them.

Lake Michigan and Michigan Avenue bear an Algonquin name, "Great Water"; Ontario Street means "Beautiful Lake"; Ohio Street, "Beautiful River"; Saginaw, "Mouth of the River." Calumet, the Indian word for peace pipe, is carried on by a street, a high school, a river, and a harbor.

6.   A FORT AND A MASSACRE

A SULTRY blanket of heat hung over the marshy lands of Chicago. The greenish-brown river seemed almost dead. A sand bar choking its mouth forced it to curve half a mile to the south before it could enter the lake. Hundreds of Indians watched silently from low sand dunes as a company of blue-coated men, hair in pigtails, pitched their tents near the river. They had come on foot from Detroit, every step reported by Indian scouts. They, too, watched as a "canoe with big wings," the sloop *Tracy,* came into view. It carried their commanding officer, Captain John Whistler, his family, and all their provisions.

It was August 17, 1803. On orders from General Henry Dearborn, United States Secretary of War, these men were to build a new wilderness fort. It would bear the name Fort Dearborn.

Curiosity took the Indians close to the shore as the sloop was unloaded. Captain Whistler learned from a trader that the Potawatomi were one thousand warriors strong and could muster five hundred allies. His own men numbered sixty-six besides officers and a handful of civilians. The fort must be built quickly.

Men were sent to the scrub-oak forests to fell trees, but work was slow. The heat was intense. The mosquitoes were fierce. There were not enough saws and not enough men to finish the logs. Without oxen, men themselves had to get into harness to pull the great logs through the marshes.

Fall passed. Snow fell. Bitter winds from the lake were harder to bear than the heat. The fort still was unfinished in the summer of 1804 when a new trader, John Kinzie, moved his family into Du Sable's cabin. Men at the fort needed clothing. There was not enough food.

John Kinzie was Scots, a trader in furs and a skilled silversmith. His arm bands and buckles were prized by the Indians. In a short time he had persuaded his Indian friends to bring corn, game, and needed supplies for the fort. Some brought loaded canoes down the lake from Fort Mackinac.

Fort Dearborn, built according to Whistler's

Chicago Historical Society

THE FIRST FORT DEARBORN. A MODEL BY A. L. VAN DEN BERGHEN FROM
A DRAWING BY CAPTAIN WHISTLER

own plans, had two blockhouses, three cannons, and a stand of small arms. The main gate faced south, flanked by barracks and a hospital. Officers' barracks, a stone powder magazine, a contractor's store, and a storehouse faced the inner parade grounds. A twelve-foot stockade circled the fort. A covered way, guarding a well, led to the river.

For nine years the Stars and Stripes whipped in the wind from its pole in the center of the stockade. All seemed peaceful. Soldiers kept up a dull round of drills and work, with plenty of time for hunting and fishing.

But once more Chief Tecumseh, backed by the

British, began urging tribes to rise up against settlers. Once more the young United States government was ready to declare war with the British.
All American forts on the lakes were in danger.

In August of 1812 a runner brought orders
from General Hull in Detroit to Fort Dearborn's
new captain, Nathan Heald. Heald was told to
dispose of supplies and evacuate the fort, moving
his men to Detroit or Fort Wayne. News spread
on the wind and, from all sides, Indians moved toward the fort.

Kinzie urged Captain Heald to delay his de-
parture, but Heald did not welcome advice from a
trader. Calling a meeting, he asked Potawatomi
chiefs to supply a "safe-conduct guard." In return
for the guard, the young captain promised to give
all supplies that remained in the fort. He spoke
without thinking. Others told him how danger-
ous it would be to give all the firearms, powder,
and whisky to the Indians.

That night Captain Heald told his men to
dump all such supplies in the river. He had for-
gotten his promise. But the red men who silently
watched by the river had not.

The next morning Chief Black Partridge, long
friendly to Kinzie and white men, called at the
fort to return the medal he had received from the

United States government. He told Captain
Heald that no one could control the angry young
warriors. He himself had no choice. He must stay
with his Indian brothers. He no longer could
wear the medal from white men.

Captain William Wells, a veteran Indian fighter
who had come from Fort Wayne with a guard of
Miami, warned Captain Heald of great danger.
Captain Heald once again read his orders from
Hull.

On the morning of August 15 the gates of the
fort were thrown open. Potawatomi warriors, the
"safe-conduct" guard, silently sat on their horses.
Captain Wells and his Miami scouts, faces blackened for trouble, were the first to walk out. The
fort's band marched out, playing Handel's "Dead
March." The troops marched behind, followed by
officers' wives and twelve children, who rode in a
wagon.

John Kinzie put his own wife and children in
charge of friendly Indians. They were to leave for
Saint Joseph by boat. Kinzie would march with
the soldiers, hoping to guard his step-daughter,
Margaret, wife of Lieutenant Helm. As he moved
into line, John Kinzie did not know that his wife
and the Indians had hidden their boat in tall
grasses.

Riding south on what is now Michigan Avenue, Captain Wells saw heads "popping like turtles in water" above the low dunes. He raced his horse back to warn Captain Heald. His scouts simply vanished. The Potawatomi "safe-conduct" guard disappeared in the dunes, and some three hundred warriors swarmed down on the soldiers with blood-curdling yells.

Many were killed in the first round of bullets. Crazed Indians rushed toward the women and children, scalping and whooping. Captain Wells fought with such fury that, when he and his horse were finally shot down, two Indians paused to cut out his heart. They ate it, hoping to gain some small part of his courage.

Black Partridge saved Mrs. Helm, snatching her back as a tomahawk flew at her head. He carried her down to the river and the hidden boat. John Kinzie also was rescued by Indian friends. Mrs. Heald, badly wounded, was purchased from her captor and carried to the boat.

Captain Heald and a handful of men gained a low hill. Indians sent a demand to surrender. The captain offered one hundred dollars for every life spared, but the wounded already were doomed for long torture and others were dragged off to slavery. Of the ninety-five whites who marched

MEMORIAL TO THE FORT DEARBORN MASSACRE WITH THE CHICAGO
TRIBUNE TOWER IN THE BACKGROUND

from the fort, there were forty-three left. Twelve children were killed.

On the southwest pillar of the Michigan Avenue Bridge today there is a sculptured story of this tragic chapter in Chicago's history. In the Chicago Historical Society there is a small leather trunk with a wedding comb and silver teaspoons that once belonged to Captain Heald's wife. They were found in Saint Louis years after the massacre.

7. MUDHOLE TO BOOM TOWN

SETTLERS in the Northwest Territory still needed protection from Indians, and Captain Hezekiah Bradley was sent with a company of soldiers to rebuild Fort Dearborn in July 1816.

Trader John Kinzie returned to his home on the north bank of the river. The government built a house for its Indian agent outside the fort, and the American Fur Company sent a French fur trader, Jean Baptiste Beaubien, to live near the fort with his Indian wife and thirteen children.

Still, Chicago was only a dot in the wilderness. When Illinois applied for statehood in 1818, the portage and fort were left outside the boundaries of the new state. In time Chicago would have become part of Wisconsin. But Nathaniel Pope, territorial delegate from Illinois, shared Joliet's ancient dream of a lake-river trade route. He per-

suaded Congress to move the Illinois boundaries
forty-one miles north of the southern tip of Lake
Michigan so that an eventual canal would connect
the new state with Lake Michigan. Pope believed
that trade created by a canal route would help
Illinois to prosper. It was important for all Northwest lands to grow rich in order to offset the power
that wealthy southern states held in the government of the United States.

Many scoffed at the idea of a canal and a town
at the Chicago portage. "It could never become a
place of business," Major Long said when he sur-
veyed Northwest lands for the government. "Chicago has no harbor, no lake cargo, no agriculture.
Even the Indians will soon leave."

Nearly everyone expected Milwaukee, Wisconsin, or Michigan City, Indiana, to become the gateway to new lands in the North and West. But
another Illinois delegate to Congress, Daniel P.
Cook, believed that Chicago was the true gateway.
He persuaded the United States Government to set
aside 224,333 acres of land, a strip ten miles wide
from La Salle, Illinois, to Chicago, for a canal.
Cook County later was named for this man of long
vision.

A canal commission was established in 1830,
and surveyor James Thompson was sent to map

the village at the fork of the Chicago River. It covered three eighths of a square mile, bounded by present-day Madison, State, Kinzie, and Des Plaines streets. Thompson's map, filed August fourth, was the first to recognize the existence of Chicago. Only fifty people lived outside the fort. Few others were expected to come. Still one man knew at first glance that he wanted to live near the Chicago portage. Young Gordon Saltonstall Hubbard, an apprentice for the American Fur Company, waded ashore from a Mackinac boat in 1818, and climbed a tall tree to get his bearings. The beauty of the country filled him with excitement. A sea of tall grasses rippled in the sun. Ducks, geese, swans, brant, and teal rose in swarms from the marshes. A flag fluttered over Fort Dearborn. Hubbard did not visit the fort that day but went with fellow traders across the mud portage. Logs had to be rolled under the boat so that it could be pushed ahead. Men waded waist-deep in the mud. Hubbard was covered with leeches when he finally crawled to dry land, but his spirits were high, and he announced that Chicago would be his future home. Twelve years later he bought his first acres of land in the village, paying $67 for them. In five years he sold his land for $96,700. A street is named Hubbard today.

In 1831 the garrison was ordered to leave Fort Dearborn, for the Indian scares were thought to be over. But the following year Chief Black Hawk was back on the warpath, and settlers flocked to the fort.

General Winfield Scott arrived from Detroit on the *Sheldon Thompson,* first steamboat to reach Chicago. But cholera, a disease more feared than red warriors, kept him from following Black Hawk. Fort Dearborn became a hospital. So many men died that a common grave was dug near present-day Lake Street and Wabash Avenue. Before Scott could reach Black Hawk's territory, the Illinois militia defeated the chief in the last great Illinois Indian battle.

On August 4, 1833, taxpayers voted to make Chicago a village. It had forty-three houses, a log jail, and two hundred inhabitants, including a butcher, a gunsmith, a miller, a blacksmith, a preacher, a mail rider, a teacher, and many storekeepers.

Eighteen citizens turned out on August ninth to elect village trustees and pass laws. One law said, "No hog is to run at large without a ring in its nose or a yoke about its neck. Owners will be fined two dollars." But the law did not stop cows and pigs, as well as sheep and geese, from roaming

STATUE BY IVAN MESTROVIC IN GRANT PARK

the streets freely.

Chicago had hardly been declared a village when Colonel Owen, Indian agent at Chicago, called Indian chiefs to a powwow on the banks of the river. He had been ordered to tell the defeated tribes that the United States Government had decided to move them west of the Mississippi River.

Five thousand warriors arrived with their squaws, their children, their ponies and dogs. It was September 1833. Campfires blazed in a great circle around the small village.

Colonel Owen spoke in a roundabout way. "The Great White Father in Washington has heard that the Indians wish to sell their lands," he began.

An old chief solemnly rose to his feet and replied, "The Great White Father has listened to a bad bird. The Indians have no wish to sell their lands."

Colonel Owen then spoke plainly. He said that the government insisted on buying the Indians' lands.

The old chief looked up at the sky. "The weather is not clear enough for so solemn a council," he said, and for many days the Indians could not be persuaded to meet again.

"The village was in an uproar both day and night," one citizen wrote. "The Indians howled, sang, wept, yelled, and whooped all night long. And the whites were as pagan as the red men."

All day long the elder chiefs sat under the trees, talking of ways to keep their lands. They put off the meeting as long as they could. But on September 25 a cannon boomed from Fort Dearborn and they knew that further delay was impossible. The chiefs signed the treaty that allowed the United States Government to buy five million acres of Middle Western land.

Two years later Indians gathered once more in Chicago to collect the last payment and hold their last dance on ancestral lands. Many were dressed for the warpath. Citizens shivered. Some said that the Indians' dances would soon lead to bloodshed. Only a few knew that the hundreds of warriors on the banks of the river were performing a funeral dance, a bitter farewell to their long-traveled portage. Then, folding their wigwams, the Indians turned their ponies' heads toward the west. Chicago and Illinois lands were left to white settlers.

Suddenly the whole country went land-mad. Men made their fortunes buying Indian lands at government auctions, reselling them for all they could get. Land had no fixed value in Chicago, and many fortunes were made overnight. Men from cities and towns in the East poured into Chicago.

The Wright family stopped for supplies in Chicago before moving on farther west. Seventeen-year-old John Stephen Wright heard of an auction of government land and bought two lots for ten dollars. In a few weeks he sold them for one thousand dollars. In two years he had made $200,000 and had decided to live in Chicago. The young village boomed.

Stagecoaches filled with land buyers began to arrive twice a week from Detroit. Chicago's taverns, "Rat Castle," "Wolf Tavern," and "The Sauganash," were crowded with speculators, traders, Indians, horse thieves, and young men looking for a chance to make money fast. Lawyers earned as much as five hundred dollars a day making out land titles. Storekeepers prospered.

John Calhoun, a young printer, started Chicago's first newspaper, the Chicago *Democrat*. A brick house was built for John Noble, a man from Saint Louis who, just one year before, had been unable to find Chicago because of tall prairie grasses. Henry Whitehead built the first store on State Street. The present world-famous street of big department stores was half under water at the time.

Chicago's future as a slaughterhouse-meat-packing center was forecast when George W. Dole sent a schooner loaded with two hundred and eighty-seven barrels of beef, fourteen barrels of tallow, and 152 cowhides off through Lake Michigan.

The port of Chicago was born when army en-

gineer Jefferson Davis persuaded Congress to vote
$25,000 for cutting through the sand bar that
choked the mouth of the Chicago River. For years
the river had been forced to turn south, entering
the lake at present-day Madison Street. With the
cutting through of the sand bar, the river could
flow straight into the lake and a deep harbor could
be dredged.

STATE AND MADISON STREETS IN 1905

Chicago Historical Society

By 1835 Chicago had seventy-five buildings and a population of nine thousand. Two thousand more men walked the mud streets, looking for jobs and waiting to buy the right piece of land. More and more men came to Chicago on foot and on horseback. A few came by canals and by lakes. Families rode in ox-drawn wagons from New York, Pennsylvania, Ohio, Virginia. They came from Kentucky and Indiana—some with fine furnishings, some with only the barest necessities. Some were highly educated; some had no "book learning" at all.

Harriet Martineau visited Chicago in 1836 and wrote about "educated and wealthy persons" who lived in small houses on the edge of a wild prairie. One house held a piano, yet wolves still entered the village. Dances were held in log houses with dancers in deerskin jackets and ball gowns. If anyone shouted, "Bear!" every man seized his gun and went hunting.

8. GIANTS STRIDE

A STRANGE lot of giants moved into Chicago between 1840 and 1870. They brought wits and youthful ambition to their new home. They were daring, ingenious, impatient with trifles. Mud, fire, floods, and panics all failed to stop them from building a city as they built their own fortunes. "I will" was their motto.

William B. Ogden brought nine hundred Irish and eight hundred Germans to Chicago in 1836. They were to dig "the big ditch," the long-talked-of Illinois and Michigan Canal. On July 4, throngs of Chicagoans boarded flag-bedecked barges and schooners for a holiday in Lockport. There Simon Archer set off a singing, shouting, firecracker celebration by throwing out the first spadeful of dirt for the canal. Now, everyone said, Chicago was sure to grow big and rich.

77

Mr. Ogden himself had grown rich selling land in Chicago. He had come from New York to look over land that an uncle had bought, sight unseen. The lots, he soon found, were half under water and apparently good for nothing. Nevertheless young Ogden set out to drain them. To his surprise, the lots sold at auction for $100,000. Instead of returning to his home in the East, he stayed in the village. He became not only a real

A STEAMBOAT USED IN BUILDING THE ILLINOIS AND MICHIGAN CANAL. FROM A WATERCOLOR BY W. E. S. TROWBRIDGE

Chicago Historical Society

estate king but a canal builder, a railroad mag-
nate, and Chicago's first mayor.

John Stephen Wright and many others lost their
quickly made fortunes, but not their spirits.
Mayor Ogden borrowed money on his own property to pay the city's bills. "Bankruptcy is a dis-
grace," he told his councilmen. John Wright
started a newspaper for farmers, whose cattle and
corn and hogs were to become the city's true
wealth. He wrote dozens of pamphlets telling men
"back East" and in Europe of the great opportuni-
ties for wealth and good living in the city on the
lake. His glowing words encouraged thousands of
families to leave old homes and start new ones in
Chicago.

Chicago was incorporated as a city on March 4,
1837. That year financial panic swept the whole
country, and all business seemed to stop. Banks
failed. The state of Illinois went bankrupt. Land
buyers vanished, and Chicago's inns were empty.

Two hundred and fifty wagons a day struggled
into Chicago but did not stay. The land was "no
good for farming," men said. "Just jump up and
down on it and you'll soon know it's a bottomless
marsh."

Chicago became known as no more than a stop-
ping-off place for supplies. It remained a village

while 50,000 new settlers went to farming within sixty miles. The city's merchants talked of ways to keep settlers' trade even if they didn't stay in town. If the roads were not a vast sea of mud in wet weather, these new settlers would return to Chicago to trade hogs and farm crops for supplies. As it was, one hundred and sixty wagons were stuck deep in the mud at one time, just outside Chicago. Chicagoans set out to build roads on which wagons could travel.

It looked like a hopeless job at first. Grass grew higher than men's heads on the prairies. Underfoot were the marsh and the mud. But Chicago's young giants rolled up their sleeves and laid mile after mile of huge logs side by side along Indian trails. But logs sank into mud as quickly as wagons. The men next laid logs end to end and placed thick planks across them. Spiked together, the logs and planks held firm. The Barry Point, the Blue Island, and Western Plank roads soon led out of the city. Two hundred wagons a day began to bump into Chicago. Seventy thousand wagons reached town in one year, bringing corn, oats, and soybeans, onions, potatoes, apples, and poultry. They returned home filled with salt, tar, cloth, and lumber for building. Drivers paid fees for each trip on the plank roads and the tolls repaid builders who had boldly invested their money.

But mud was still deep in Chicago itself. The streets, only two feet above the river level, were flooded with each heavy rain. Wealthy citizens moved to land slightly higher, north and south, but poor people lived in cottages propped up on stilts.

Miles and miles of board sidewalks were built over mud. Owners of houses and stores each chose the height for the sidewalks they built. Some were six feet, some only two feet high. Ladders and steps joined the walks. As people walked up and down, they looked much like puppets bouncing in a jack-in-the-box show. Many fell and broke bones.

The mud was so bad that people made jokes about it. Signs were stuck up in streets saying, "No Bottom Here," and cartoons in newspapers showed ladies in hoop skirts falling from high walks, disappearing "under full sail" in the mud.

One traveler told a tall tale about seeing a good hat floating in mud. He reached down to get it and, to his surprise, found a man under it.

"Do you need help?" the traveler cried loudly.

"No thanks," said the man in the mud. "I have a good horse under me."

Chicago itself had to rise from the mud before it could grow.

Giants who liked to say, "Nothing is impossible," decided to lift city streets to a height that would defy rain and floods. Houses and shops would then need to be lifted.

In 1858 the fashionable Tremont House seemed to be sinking clear out of sight when a young man named George Pullman walked into town. Pullman offered to raise the five-story brick hotel six feet without shaking one glass on a dining-room table.

He placed two thousand five hundred jackscrews under the building. At a signal five hundred men each turned five screws and, slowly but surely, the hotel inched upward. Owners of buildings all over Chicago began bidding for the new giant's services. George H. Pullman later became a multimillionaire, making sleeping cars for the railroads. The town which he built for his workers south of Chicago is now part of the city itself.

There are still blocks in Chicago where gardens and ground floors of houses are lower than street level. Bridges cross from houses to streets. Steps lead down to front yards and up to second-story front doors.

It took twelve years to build the Illinois and Michigan Canal, but in 1848 Joliet's dream of connecting the Atlantic Ocean with the Gulf of Mexico came true. At once barges, schooners,

THE "MADEIRA PET" FROM LIVERPOOL IN 1857

brigs, and side-wheelers crowded the new canal. They carried passengers, lumber, sugar, cotton, and thousands of bushels of corn. Boats reached the city much faster than wagons.

Storage elevators for grain, a Chicago invention, began to tower on the banks of the Chicago River. Grain was held through the winter while ice choked the lakes. In spring the grain was sent east on lake schooners. Six million bushels left Chicago in 1853. Twelve million bushels went out in 1856, and Chicago was well on its way to becoming the biggest grain market in the world.

Shipping of all kinds boomed in Chicago. By 1857 seventy-seven ships on regular schedules were passing the lighthouse at the mouth of the river each forty-eight hours. They carried millions of feet of lumber from northern forests. Lumberyards on the river were stacked thirty feet high. New giants grew rich owning warehouses, grain elevators, ships, coal and lumberyards.

Most lumber was used for Chicago's own houses, and the young city was nicknamed "Slab Town." But lumber also was sent to the prairies. One firm even started to make prefabricated houses, stores, schools, and churches.

Because Chicago was such a fast-growing city, men were forced to invent many new building methods. One, called "balloon framing," was devised in 1837 by George Washington Snow. It is still the world's standard method of building inexpensive houses. Boards are nailed together to form a slat cage. Any type of material may then be used inside and out.

In all of its years of growing, Chicago has claimed many building "firsts." It was first to discover fireproof materials; first to use steel grilles that gave solid footing for building on marshy lands; first to build steel-skeleton skyscrapers. The ten-story Home Insurance Building, designed by William Le Baron Jenny in 1885, set off a new era in building.

FLOODLIGHTED BUILDINGS MAKE THE CITY BRILLIANT AT NIGHT

Many of Chicago's first giants were inventors. Cyrus H. McCormick invented the reaper that helped Chicago grow with new speed. Steel plows already had helped farmers cut through the deep-matted sod of the Illinois prairies. The reaper revolutionized the cutting of grain and sent millions of bushels into Chicago for shipment and sale.

McCormick invented his reaper in Virginia but chose Chicago, "ugliest and youngest of cities," as a place to manufacture it. In Chicago he could assemble wood, iron, and steel from many places. He could ship finished machines quickly and cheaply. Needing money to build his first factory, Cyrus McCormick turned to canal-builder Ogden and borrowed $25,000. In two years he returned $50,000, the loan plus an added $25,000 profit.

McCormick's method of selling his reapers was as revolutionary as the reaper itself. He insisted that the price of a reaper must be the same to every farmer: "Thirty dollars down; ninety dollars in six months. Take it or leave it." There was no bargaining and each reaper was guaranteed to be perfect.

Businessmen said that McCormick was mad. Didn't everyone bargain and take the best price he could get? And who guaranteed anything? It was up to the buyer to keep his eyes peeled.

McCormick went even further. He trusted the farmer to pay in six months, and in spite of all warnings, he did not lose money. Farmers paid their bills and the reapers themselves became their own salesmen.

When thousands of men left farms for the gold fields of California in 1849, McCormick's business boomed. Each reaper proved it could do the work of many men. Reapers helped the wheat states to defeat the cotton states during the Civil War. In 1884, the year McCormick died, he was still working in his office every day. Like all of Chicago's rich giants, he never could quit. "The richer men are in Chicago, the harder they work," eastern visitors said. McCormick answered for all the young city's workers when he said, "I don't know of a better way to die than in harness."

As Chicago kept growing, other cities grew jealous. Their newspapers predicted that Chicago's boom would collapse in a breeze like a deck of cards. But one young man from Kentucky, a world traveler, looked at the city and said, "I think Chicago is destined to be the greatest city on the continent. I have decided to cast my lot with it." He was Carter H. Harrison, a man who became one of Chicago's most popular mayors.

Chicago had one big handicap, however, which kept it from growing as fast as it could. Its trade depended almost entirely on north-south shipping through lakes, canals, and rivers. Rivers often

were too shallow for heavily laden boats. Waters
of lakes and rivers were frozen part of the year.
Chicago needed a network of railroads to give it
control of Midwest commerce and put its business
ahead of Saint Louis and Cincinnati.

William Ogden had dreamed of connecting
Chicago with the East by rail even before he
started to build the Illinois and Michigan Canal,
but no one had shared his dreams. Just before the
canal was completed in 1848, he tried once again
to interest bankers and merchants in a new railroad. Still no one wished to invest any money, and
many merchants even thought that a railroad
would keep Chicago from growing.

"Farmers will stop coming if they can ship all
their products by railroad," they said. "Grass will
grow in the streets of the city."

Stagecoach owners, who feared competition
from the railroads said, "Locomotives will scare all
the cows so they won't give down their milk at
night. A railroad will harm all our farmers."

Some people simply laughed at the idea of "fire-
eating monsters." How could they take the place
of good horses? Everyone, millionaires to butcher
boys, owned horses. Horses pulled fashionable
carriages, delivery trucks, fire trucks, and stagecoaches. Hotels were built with stables for one

hundred or more horses. Who could do without horses?

William Ogden had no time for discouraging talk. He hitched his own horse to a buggy and set out to raise money for his railroad. He went straight to rich farmers, offering shares of stock for only a few dollars. He even offered "a chance to pay later when your money comes in from your crops." Farmers bought hundreds of shares of railroad stock. Their wives even reached into old stockings where savings were hidden and bought stock for themselves and their children. Ogden started to build the Galena and Chicago Union Railroad. Secondhand rails were laid down as far west as the Des Plaines River. Later, the railroad was called the Chicago and Northwestern.

A secondhand engine, the little wood-burning Pioneer, arrived on the deck of a freighter, and on November 20, 1848, Mr. Ogden invited a group of Chicago businessmen to ride behind his iron horse in a crude baggage car. The Pioneer puffed stoutly along over eight miles of track. As it passed a wagonload of grain, one passenger begged Mr. Ogden to stop. Buying the grain, he had it dumped into the baggage car. Later he boasted that he had made the first shipment of grain into Chicago.

In its first year the Galena and Chicago Union Railroad earned $2000 a month hauling farm products. In its second year it earned $9000 a month. Farmers who had bought shares in the railroad became wealthy men. Faith in railroads shot up like a fever thermometer. Even eastern bankers began to buy stock in Middle-Western railroads.

Senators Stephen A. Douglas and Sidney Breese persuaded Congress to give 2,595,000 acres of land for a second railroad between Chicago and Cairo, Illinois, the point where the Ohio River meets the Mississippi. It was the first such railroad grant in the new world, and the Illinois Central Railroad was born.

The new railroad asked to purchase the site of Fort Dearborn from the city of Chicago. In return for land rights, it agreed to build walls to protect Michigan Avenue, which was being cut back by Lake Michigan's waves. Tracks were laid from Randolph Street toward the south, crossing the lake on trestles where Grant Park now spreads its carpet of grass. A lagoon separated tracks from Michigan Avenue.

Chicago's lake front might never have grown into a beautiful playground if one man, A. Montgomery Ward, giant of the mail-order business,

GREAT RAILWAY STATION AT CHICAGO. AN ENGRAVING FROM APPLETON'S JOURNAL

had not stepped into the battle. More than forty buildings cluttered the new land between the river and Jackson Boulevard when Ward started to urge the city to "keep the lake front for the people." It took thousands of dollars, years of time, and a tireless spirit to win the battle, but the lake front was cleared of old buildings. Railroad tracks were submerged and Grant Park was planted with trees. Today the Art Institute is the only building east of Michigan Avenue between Randolph and Twelfth streets. When the Art Institute built the Goodman Memorial Theater, it was placed under ground with only a shell of an entrance above ground.

A network of railroad tracks began to surround the city in the 1850s. Eleven trunk lines and seventeen branch lines ran into the city by 1856. There were frequent wrecks as trains raced along at the high speed of thirty miles per hour. Many engines jumped the track or toppled over after crashing into cows. Each engine had its own "cow-catcher," and section hands were instructed "to clear the tracks of all beasts one hour before train time." But still there were wrecks. Some were caused by stubborn engineers themselves. Like many other Chicago giants, they rushed full speed ahead with little regard for others. There were no signals at intersections, and no rules of fair play. Newspaper headlines told lurid tales of collisions in which many passengers were crippled and killed.

Still, swift transportation became the talk of the country, and women from farms and small towns grew more and more eager to ride on the trains and to shop in Chicago's beautiful stores. Men and women both wanted to visit the fairs that Chicago kept holding, and 5000 rode into the city in eighty-four coaches for the first day of the 1859 Agricultural Fair.

Railroads made it possible for the young Republican party to hold the 1860 convention in

THE WIGWAM FROM A DRAWING IN "HARPER'S WEEKLY" MAY 19, 1860

Chicago. Chicago built the "Wigwam" for the convention, with seats for 10,000 people and standing room for 4000 more.

One wealthy group was determined to nominate William H. Seward, "a man from the East," who wore fine clothes. But thousands wanted Abe Lincoln, "a plain Northwest man" like themselves. These men had no money for hiring brass bands, but they had "wits to burn and more determination than all outdoors." While Seward's men marched with their bands in the streets, exciting the crowds, Lincoln's men packed the Wigwam. They left almost no seats for opponents. When Seward's name was presented, there were few of his followers inside the Wigwam to cheer. But when Lincoln was nominated, his men uttered earsplitting yells "like the unbridled shrieks of Indians on the warpath."

That night Lincoln's men, "the Wide-Awakes," held a torchlight parade with flaming barrels of pitch, and lanterns strung on fence rails. They wore white oilcloth capes and marched shoulder to shoulder, singing, "Old Abe Lincoln came out of the wilderness."

As Chicago grew, its reputation as "butcher" spread over the country. Farmers drove thundering herds of cattle into Chicago. The cattle pounded across the river's narrow bridges, plowed up its streets, and started cyclones of dust in dry seasons. "Yards," where cattle were held until they could be driven to slaughterhouses, were on the edges of town. Slaughterhouses lined the river. Finally, owners of railroads and yards decided to set up the Union Stock Yards, where all animals could be delivered.

The stockyards were opened on Christmas Day, 1865, several miles south of the river's "Y" stem. Three hundred and forty-five acres of swampland had been drained. Wells had been dug for pure water. Seven miles of streets and alleys had been paved with wooden blocks. There were pens for 118,200 animals. The new animal town was cleaner and more sanitary than Chicago itself, but its stench swept over the city with every strong breeze.

The packing business reached new heights when the refrigerated car was invented and meat could be sent to distant cities by railroad. Business jumped ahead again when new uses were discovered for all parts of the animal. A new crop of millionaires rose, whose companies made saddles and harness for horses; boots and shoes for men, women, and children; soap, candles, glue, fertilizers, and many important medicines.

By the end of the Civil War Chicago had grown from a frontier town to a metropolis. By 1870 it was the second-largest city in the United States, with almost 300,000 people. Carl Sandburg described Chicago as:

> Hog Butcher for the world
> Tool Maker, Stacker of Wheat,
> Player with Railroads and the Nation's
>   Freight Handler;
> Stormy, husky, brawling
> City of the Big Shoulders.

"Even our millionaires are workingmen," Chicagoans boasted. "They came without money and built their own fortunes. They built a city with jobs and opportunity for everyone. Nothing can keep Chicago from growing bigger and richer and stronger."

No one knew that fire was waiting to level Chicago.

9. FIRE!

In 1871 forty thousand of Chicago's estimated sixty thousand houses were built of wood, though a few elegant houses and stores had faces of brick, iron, or marble. Fires were everyday happenings. Young men belonged to volunteer fire companies that fought fires and one another like rival football teams. No one seemed to worry about fire laws, but the Chicago *Tribune* kept warning, "This city holds miles of firetraps, pleasing to the eye but all sham and shingles."

The summer and early fall had been unusually dry. In the first few days of October, thirty fires set alarm bells to ringing. On October seventh a lumber mill burned, taking four solid blocks of buildings with it. Every fire company in town turned out, fighting for sixteen hours, until men were exhausted and half their equipment destroyed. Yet before they could sleep, a fire that was to shock the whole world started blazing.

It began on Sunday evening, October eighth. The story goes that Mrs. O'Leary's cow kicked over a lantern, but no one really knows how the fire started. It is only known that the fire spread for two hours before anyone was on hand to fight it. By midnight it had swept half a mile and jumped the south branch of the river. From plants on the river it spread to the heart of the business district. There flames spread to the Courthouse, and that sturdy-looking building burned in fifteen minutes. Men began to hurry from their homes on Michigan Avenue and north of the river to be near their stores and offices "just in case the fire spread." It spread fast.

Suddenly the whole city seemed to be burning. Walls of flame moved from building to building. Streets were filled with frantic people, some with clothing on fire, falling and trampling one another. Panic swept like the fire. Rush Street Bridge was a bedlam of horses, wagons, and desperate people carrying children and bundles. The stationary bridge at State Street burned as the fire leaped to the McCormick reaper works.

People who lived in brick mansions on the north side of the river could not believe that the fire could reach them. But whirling showers of sparks and flame moved high in the air to start fires far beyond the main one. Some said the wind fanned the flames, but the whirling masses were "fire devils," superheated air generated and tossed not by wind, but by the fire itself.

Homes melted in less than ten minutes. Men timed them, holding watches and staring in dismay. Those who had gone "just to take a look" rushed home to tell families to pack whatever they could and move quickly. Children worked with parents to bury silver and valuable possessions. Some even buried pianos, but nothing survived the searing heat of the ruins that covered the ground.

Those who had horses and carriages drove to friends in the country. Some caught loose horses racing from burning stables. Streets were jammed with people dragging bundles by ropes, pushing loaded wheelbarrows, hauling wagons and carts. Dogs, chickens, and bellowing cows with scorched backs rammed through crowds. Children were lost. Men who went to help others did not return.

Millionaires and their families fared no better than the poorest families in town. Some nearly lost their lives trying to save valuable paintings and furnishings.

Thousands waded into the lake as the fire pressed on them. Some stood waist-deep in water for fourteen hours or more. Only a few could get into boats. Piers sagged with their loads of terror-stricken people. Lincoln Park, at the north edge of the city, became a refuge for countless thousands. More thousands fought their way to the prairies west of the city.

As they went, many paused to leave valuable possessions at the Chicago Historical Society. But this building also burned to the ground with its entire collection of early newspapers, maps, photographs, manuscripts, letters, paintings, and valuable relics of early Chicago. Sam Stone, the assistant librarian made a heroic effort to save President Lincoln's famous Emancipation Proclamation that had freed the slaves. Lincoln had given it to Chicago in October 1863, to be sold at a benefit for needy soldiers. But Sam could not tear the heavy wood frame from the wall. The entire building was in flames before he rushed out to save his own life.

Sometime near midnight on Monday, October ninth, rain started. It checked the twenty-seven-hour inferno only slightly and brought added misery to refugees, many of whom wore only night clothes.

AUGUSTUS ST. GAUDENS' STATUE OF LINCOLN IN LINCOLN PARK

On the morning of October tenth Chicago lay smoldering. Ninety-eight thousand people were homeless. Many were known dead. No one knew how many were missing. Thirty-six hundred and fifty buildings were gone. The city lay twisted and broken in masses of iron, charred cement, blackened stone, and hot cinders.

On the north side one big frame house stood
like a desolate orphan in acres of ruins. Newberry
Library stands on this site today. The Water
Tower, whose machinery had been put out of
business in the early hours of the fire, stood alone,
its castellated head held high. The O'Leary cot-
tage (no one could believe it) stood unharmed in
blocks of black ruin.

The fire remains one of the great tragedies of
the nineteenth century. Its story has been told in
hundreds of books, pamphlets, personal letters,
photographs, and paintings.

As the news spread, reporters and artists from
newspapers in every city over the country rushed
to Chicago. They stayed weeks to record tales of
heroism and cowardice, of sacrifice and courage.
They told how people kept on living after they had
lost all. Those who fled from the fire had nothing.
Shoes, clothing, forks, spoons, all personal and
household necessities were gone, down to the last
safety pin.

There was no water, no gas, no tools for rebuild-
ing. Ten companies of regular infantry and seven
companies of militia from neighboring towns
helped to patrol the city and stop looting.

Relief stations were set up to feed people. Fifty
thousand army tents went up to house them. For

miles around Chicago every farmhouse, barn, and leanto sheltered the homeless. Railroads sent trains to take people out of the city without charge if they wanted to go. Forty thousand left, thinking Chicago was lost forever.

10. OUT OF THE ASHES

CHICAGO walked in a daze past the ruins of factories and stores. Men hopelessly searched smoking ruins for any small thing of the past. Then the courage and strength that had first built Chicago rose like a tide in thousands of hearts.

William Kerfoot, a real estate man, put up a sign saying, "All gone but wife, children and ENERGY." Other merchants nailed up signs that said, "We still live," "Back in business," "Keep the ball rolling."

Joseph Medill, owner of the Chicago *Tribune,* rounded up his reporters and printers. Locating a printing plant outside the fire zone, he took only two days to send out a paper whose headlines blazed their own fiery CHEER UP.

"In the midst of a calamity without parallel in the world's history, the people of this once beautiful city have resolved that Chicago shall rise again."

John Stephen Wright, the man who had spent his whole life boosting Chicago, walked with bowed head through the ruins. When someone asked bitterly, "What do you think of Chicago's future now?" the white-haired Wright, exhausted from fire fighting, looked up and said, "I will tell you what it is," and his famed spirit flashed in his eyes. "Chicago will have more men, more money, and more business within five years than she would have had without the fire."

William Bross, Wright's fellow booster, did not wait for the ashes to cool. He went to New York, inspiring men and dollars to move toward the stricken Chicago.

"Chicago is a land of opportunity," he said in his confident voice. "Once again, all men have a chance to start equal. You will never again have such a chance to make money. We are all starting over."

The whole world seemed to rush to the rescue. Saint Louis, Chicago's bitterest rival, sent fifty carloads of food and clothing within two days. Tens of thousands of dollars came, not only from friends and relatives, but from churches, schools, and every kind of group. Six hundred thousand dollars came from foreign countries. Banks and merchants everywhere offered credit to Chicago merchants. Wholesalers sent shiploads and carloads of merchandise to stores that needed everything from kitchen spoons and handkerchiefs to all kinds of furniture, clothing, and food.

The stockyards, untouched by the fire, helped to rebuild Chicago. Farmers sent more hogs and cattle than ever. They spent money in the stores that grew faster than their own corn.

THE CHICAGO PUBLIC LIBRARY

Chicago Historical Society

As shiploads of lumber and building supplies sailed into the harbor, Chicago became a great forest of derricks. In five weeks 5,497 temporary buildings were in use. One hundred thousand carpenters, masons, and workmen were raising ten thousand new buildings. No "false fronts" were allowed. Everyone talked of fireproof materials.

John Van Osdel, Chicago's first architect, had made a surprising discovery. As fire swept the center of Chicago, he had searched for a place to bury drawings of his many buildings. He dug a hole in the clay basement of the new Palmer House, which he was constructing, and covered his drawings with two feet of damp clay. The fire baked the clay, protecting the papers. After the fire, Van Osdel used fireproof clay tile in all his new buildings.

The fire spurred every ambition. Within two years Chicago had not only rebuilt thousands of homes and stores, it had built a big exposition building, "The Crystal Palace," on the site of the present Art Institute. Art shows, concerts, fairs of all kinds were to be held there. With flags flying from many masts, a fountain in the lobby, and bands playing, the palace brought praise from all kinds of visitors. It was a monument to the in- domitable spirit of Chicago. People everywhere talked about Chicago's "sleepless vitality," its "peerless faith."

The Chicago Public Library opened its doors on New Year's Day, 1873, two years after the Great Fire. Its home was an iron water tank on La Salle Street behind a temporary city hall. Thomas Hughes, author of *Tom Brown's School Days,* collected some twelve thousand books from Englishmen alone and sent them to the burned-out city.

By 1874 there were few traces of the fire. Just as Wright had predicted, there was more business and more industry than ever. There were more millionaires and more beautiful castles than ever before.

As "the phoenix city" rose from its ashes, all who had grown up in Chicago lovingly talked of the past. They remembered the terrible days of the Civil War. Chicago's own Colonel Ellsworth was the first Union officer killed in the war. His famous regiment of Zouaves had been one of the finest volunteer marching organizations in the country. Ellsworth took them down east in their bright-colored uniforms as soon as war was declared.

"Chicago was the best horse and mule market in the country during the war," men recalled. "Made the best boots and shoes, too."

Many remembered how a wealthy Chicago alderman had gone to Richmond, Virginia, shortly after the war and bought Libby Prison, where Union soldiers had been held. The prison was torn down stone by stone and reassembled in Chicago. It became a Civil War museum and a place for meetings and balls.

One favorite story concerned a rock 8 feet high that bulged in the middle. The head of an Indian Chief named Wabansa had been carved in the stone by a Fort Dearborn soldier. The stone had been hauled inside the stockade when the Fort was rebuilt in 1816. It was used as a place of punishment, and parents warned children, "You'd better not do that or you'll go to the Rock."

When the grounds of Fort Dearborn became a public park in 1865, the Wabansa stone was turned into a fountain. A millionaire, I. N. Arnold, purchased the rock and placed it in front of his mansion on Pine Street, now Michigan Avenue. During the great fire Arnold's home, with its valuable collection of paintings, was destroyed, but fire did not hurt the old stone. Some said it was guarded by the old Chief Wabansa. The Chicago Historical Society guards the stone today.

Chicago also had a great mystery which for years kept the curious talking. The first Fort Dearborn had three brass cannon. When Captain Heald ordered all arms thrown into the river, they must have gone too. At least they were not to be found when the fort was rebuilt.

Around 1850, as men dredged the mouth of the river to deepen its harbor, a derrick struck something hard and lifted a mud-covered object out of the river. Curious men washed it and knew they had found one of the ancient brass cannons. They shined it proudly and wondered where it would be displayed. They were shocked when a city marshal ordered it thrown into a junk yard. The men dumped the historic old cannon, but that night they quietly took a small boat up the river and rescued the cannon. Far up the river they transferred the cannon to a wagon and carted it off to a field, where they buried it deep in the ground. For three years they argued about how they might give the old cannon its rightful place in the city. At last they decided to sell it. It would not be safe, several thought, to let anyone know they had held the cannon so long.

Returning to the field, they opened the hole. The cannon was gone. Where had it gone? No one ever found out.

11. A RIVER RUNS BACKWARD

MANY problems plagued city officials as Chicago grew bigger. The question of "water fit to drink" was enough to give aldermen nightmares. Wealthy families bought drinking water by the barrel from wells owned by private companies, but most of Chicago's citizens drank water that came from the lake. Unfortunately the river that flowed into the lake carried all kinds of sewage and refuse. Slaughterhouses threw all the animal that was not sent to packers into the river. Lake water was black, greasy, and horrible to smell. Chicago's death rate from water-carried diseases was the highest in the nation.

It took a cholera epidemic to persuade city officials to start building sewers along streets. City boosters immediately shouted that Chicago had the first big sewer system in the country. But

111

refuse still poured into river and lake.

At last someone said, "Make the river flow backward. Let it carry the refuse away from the lake." Engineers set out to lower the channel of the Illinois and Michigan Canal eight and one-half feet. The cost was three million dollars. For one moment Chicago thought that its troubles were over.

Then owners of marshy lands south and west of

ONE OF THE BRIDGES THAT SPAN THE CHICAGO RIVER

Photo by Robert Mark, Chicago Historical Society

the city built private canals and sent torrents of water racing into the new, deepened Illinois and Michigan Canal. The ill-smelling Chicago River once more stood still in the middle of the city.

Pumps were installed and the river was forced to flow backward, but a howl arose from villages and towns along the canal. In 1889 the Illinois Legislature demanded that the giant Chicago find a new way of disposing of sewage.

This time engineers gave up halfway measures and offered a plan for scientific control of sewage through the new Sanitary and Ship Canal. By 1917 the Chicago River really flowed backward, flushed by fresh water from Lake Michigan. Suddenly the city's death rate from typhoid fever and cholera dropped to the lowest in the nation.

Water troubles were not yet over. The flow of the Little Calumet River also was reversed and cities along Lake Michigan's shores began to complain that Chicago was lowering the level of the big lake. Once again the city was ordered by the courts to reduce the amount of water taken out of Lake Michigan from ten thousand cubic feet per second to a mere fifteen hundred. The city also was ordered to build special plants for treating sewage and to have the entire job finished within eight years. No city in the world has ever been faced with a more Herculean task. But the job was completed on time and the American Society of Civil Engineers still calls Chicago's sewage treatment one of the seven engineering wonders of the world.

Today the Metropolitan Sanitary District of Greater Chicago controls seventy-one miles of navigable canals between one hundred and five villages, towns, and cities. It collects, treats, and disposes of industrial and domestic sewage from a population of more than eight million persons. It has made a color film called *Storm Warning* to explain its work to schools.

Chicago's filtration plants, the largest in the world, send pure water to all parts of the city and to dozens of neighboring towns. Every glass of drinking water has been "purged" of fish, heated, cooled, shaken, churned, and pushed through dozens of filter traps. It has been treated by eight chemicals and then deodorized.

Chicago was the first city to use electric microscopes to examine water and determine atomic fallout. It has a closed-circuit television that allows engineers in control rooms to see the condition of water at many distant spots.

12. ATOMIC AGE

A NEW AGE for all mankind began in Chicago December second, 1942. It was born in a heap of uranium in a graphite-brick pile under the stands of Stagg Field, the University of Chicago's once famous football field. There Dr. Enrico Fermi and his co-workers anxiously watched the results of a long-planned experiment. At a signal they set off the first man-made chain reaction of atomic energy. News that men could control the energy of atoms flashed over the world.

The university invited many of the world's greatest scientists to form the Fermi Institute of Nuclear Studies and to search for peacetime uses of atomic energy.

Scientific laboratories were marked out in the first plans for the university when it was founded in 1892. That year its scientists began to explore

outer space. The world's largest refractor tele-
scope was purchased and installed, not on university property, but seventy-six miles northwest of
Chicago at Williams Bay, far from the smoke and
dirt of a city.

The observatory was named for its donor,
Charles T. Yerkes, one of Chicago's early giants
who built the city's streetcar system.

Today the University of Chicago is engaged in
many kinds of scientific research. It has not only
an atom smasher, but a kevatron and a belatron
that capture the gamma rays once known only to
science fiction. University scientists have discovered a "jet stream" that affects the weather.
They also have found a "carbon dating" system of
telling the age of the earth, dating skeletons of animals, Indian arrowheads, pottery, or anything
found on the earth.

Thirteen University of Chicago scientists have
won the Nobel prize. The university was only fifteen years old when her first professor of physics,
Albert A. Michelson, became the first American to
win a Nobel prize in physics. In 1961 Willard
Libby won the Nobel prize in chemistry for de-
veloping the radioactive dating system.

The nation's greatest atomic energy laboratory,
the Argonne National Laboratory, is just twenty-
five miles from Chicago.

Fifty miles southwest of Chicago in Dresden, Illinois, there is a gigantic silver bubble, housing the world's largest nuclear reactor. From there in 1959 Commonwealth Edison Company set off a nuclear chain reaction for the production of electricity for Chicago's homes and industries.

In 1960 engineers from Illinois Bell Telephone Company headquarters in Chicago helped launch Echo, the space balloon that first transmitted human words from New Jersey to California. These engineers predict that Chicago will be the great center for space telephones.

Chicago is a center for industrial as well as for pure scientific research. Such research is as important to a growing city as workers, materials and transportation. Universities, trade associations, private companies, and special foundations support over one thousand different research organizations. They try to produce better animal feeds, fertilizers, weed killers, drugs, and vitamins; they experiment with new methods of preserving foods, of refining oil, of installing electric wires. Armour Research Foundation, the Institute of Gas Technology, and the Association of Railroads Research Center are all part of Illinois Institute of Technology. Research is as diversified in Chicago as its industries.

Medical research goes hand in hand with scientific and industrial research. Chicago is rapidly becoming the medical center of the world. Its network of hospitals, clinics, research centers, and medical schools is as intricate as its network of tracks, highways, rivers, and canals. The West Side Medical Center alone, covering three hundred and five acres, is the greatest concentration of

A MEDICAL BUILDING ON NORTHWESTERN UNIVERSITY'S DOWNTOWN CAMPUS

Chicago Historical Society

hospitals, clinics, and medical schools in the world.

One of every four doctors in the United States has had all or part of his training in one of Chicago's five great medical schools. Chicago is the only city in the world that maintains three schools for dentists, forty-four schools for nurses, and dozens of schools for technicians and specialists. Chicago is headquarters for the American Medical Association, the American Dental Association, the American Veterans' Medical Association, and the American Hospital Association.

13. MAKE NO LITTLE PLANS

"You'll never know Chicago in ten years," city boosters say as they look at a $50,000 scale model of the future downtown area.

The elevated tracks will be gone and the Loop will have a big city plaza with trees and fountains. A new court building and a new city-county building will face the plaza. There will be island playgrounds out in the lake. The river's banks will be lined with broad walks and beautiful buildings. Throughout the city there will be more parks, more ice-skating rinks, more boating areas, more outdoor theaters and places to hear music.

The sixty-story-high towers of Marina City will stand on the north bank of the river, looking down on the long modern lines of the *Sun-Times* Building, the French towers of the Wrigley Building, and the Gothic towers of the Chicago *Tribune*

A MODEL OF MARINA CITY THAT WILL RISE BESIDE THE CHICAGO RIVER

Hedrich-Blessing

Building. Marina City, financed by Federal Housing Authority and the Building Service Employees Union, will have offices, 1,120 apartments, restaurants, theaters, and parking space for boats as well as cars.

The maze of tracks owned by twelve railroads just south of the Loop will be channeled into one great railroad terminal. There will be central terminals for airport buses and countless new throughways for cars.

Chicago expects one and one half million persons to move into the city and suburbs by 1970. By 1980 it expects to have nine million residents in the metropolitan area.

Thirty million travelers a year will be passing through O'Hare International Airport by 1970. There will be new runways on Meigs Field and Chicago will be the take-off point for small planes that fly to all parts of the world.

As Chicago looks into the future, it recalls the words of architect Daniel Burnham, who made plans for a beautiful city more than fifty years ago. "Make no little plans," said Burnham. "They have no magic to stir men's souls."

Chicago's official flag flies beside the Stars and Stripes above the city hall, the courthouse, the Art Institute, and many public buildings. It is a reminder that courage and dreams have always been part of Chicago.

The flag's two blue bands honor the two branches of the Chicago River. Three white bands stand for the city's north, south, and west sides. Four red stars honor the building of Fort Dearborn in 1803; the Great Fire of 1871; the Columbian Exposition of 1893; and the Century of Progress Exposition in 1933. If the flag were remade today it would add a fifth star for 1959, when Chicago became a world inland seaport.

INDEX

125

INDEX